COUNTRY · EXPLORERS

A Visit to

AUSTRIA

By Rebecca Phillips-Bartlett

BEARPORT
PUBLISHING

Minneapolis, Minnesota

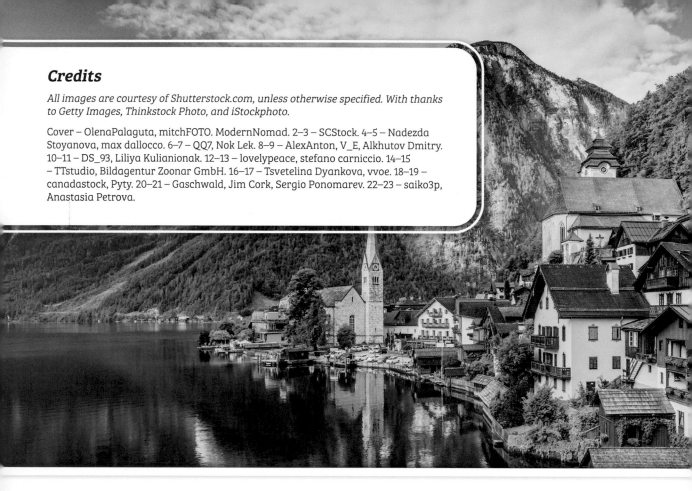

Credits

All images are courtesy of Shutterstock.com, unless otherwise specified. With thanks to Getty Images, Thinkstock Photo, and iStockphoto.

Cover – OlenaPalaguta, mitchFOTO. ModernNomad. 2–3 – SCStock. 4–5 – Nadezda Stoyanova, max dallocco. 6–7 – QQ7, Nok Lek. 8–9 – AlexAnton, V_E, Alkhutov Dmitry. 10–11 – DS_93, Liliya Kulianionak. 12–13 – lovelypeace, stefano carniccio. 14–15 – TTstudio, Bildagentur Zoonar GmbH. 16–17 – Tsvetelina Dyankova, vvoe. 18–19 – canadastock, Pyty. 20–21 – Gaschwald, Jim Cork, Sergio Ponomarev. 22–23 – saiko3p, Anastasia Petrova.

Library of Congress Cataloging-in-Publication Data is available at www.loc.gov or upon request from the publisher.

ISBN: 979-8-88509-967-7 (hardcover)
ISBN: 979-8-88822-146-4 (paperback)
ISBN: 979-8-88822-287-4 (ebook)

For more information, write to Bearport Publishing, 5357 Penn Avenue South, Minneapolis, MN 55419.

CONTENTS

COUNTRY TO COUNTRY

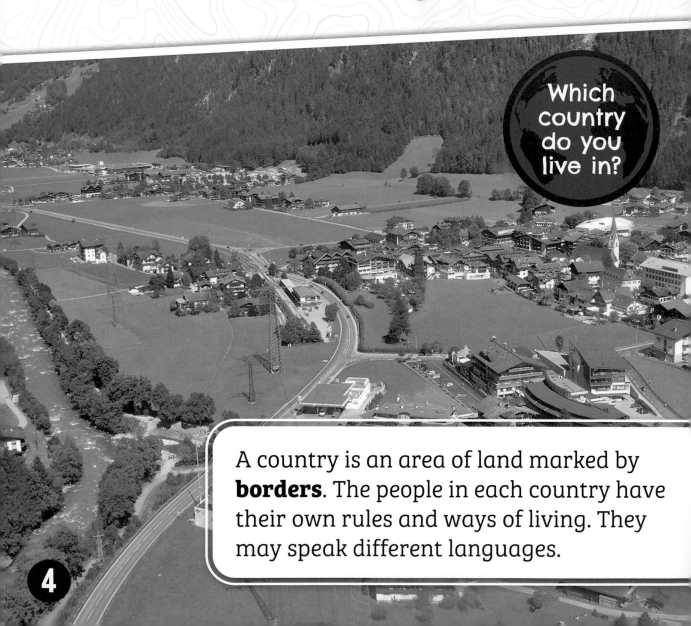

Which country do you live in?

A country is an area of land marked by **borders**. The people in each country have their own rules and ways of living. They may speak different languages.

Each country around the world has its own interesting things to see and do. Let's take a trip to visit a country and learn more!

Have you ever visited another country?

TODAY'S TRIP IS TO
AUSTRIA!

NORTH
AMERICA

SOUTH
AMERICA

Austria

EUROPE

AFRICA

ASIA

AUSTRALIA

Austria is a country in the **continent** of Europe.

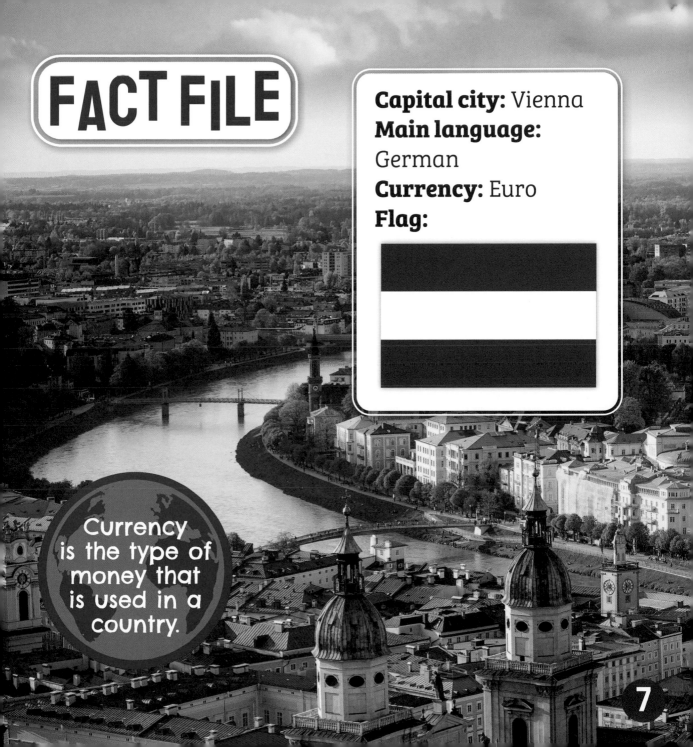

FACT FILE

Capital city: Vienna
Main language: German
Currency: Euro
Flag:

Currency is the type of money that is used in a country.

VIENNA

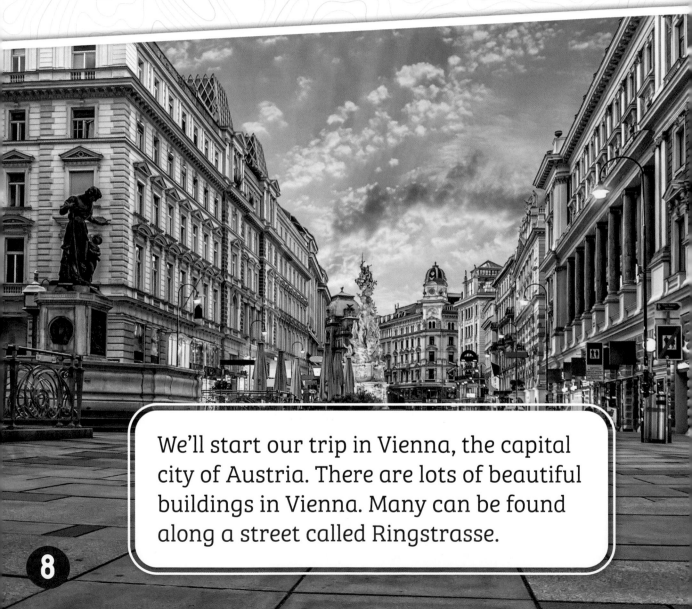

We'll start our trip in Vienna, the capital city of Austria. There are lots of beautiful buildings in Vienna. Many can be found along a street called Ringstrasse.

The cathedral roof has a colorful tile **mosaic** on it.

Vienna is home to St. Stephen's **Cathedral**. There are 13 bells inside the cathedral, including the largest bell in Austria. It weighs more than 44,000 pounds (20,000 kg)!

ART

Architecture is the art of designing buildings.

There is lots of beautiful art in Austria. One famous Austrian artist was Clemens Holzmeister. He was an **architect** famous for designing churches.

Gustav Klimt is another Austrian artist. He used the style called **symbolism**. His art had images meant to make people think of something else.

Klimt used real gold in his paintings!

MUSIC

A statue of Mozart in Vienna

Austria is also known for its history with **classical** music. The famous musician Wolfgang Amadeus Mozart lived in Austria. He started writing music when he was only five years old!

The Vienna State Opera is a great place to find classical music performances. We could watch an opera or see a ballet!

THE HOFBURG

The oldest parts of the palace are more than 800 years old.

Next, let's visit the grand Hofburg Palace. More than 100 years ago, it was the home of Austria's royal family. It is one of the biggest palaces in the world.

Today, Austria does not have a royal family. The palace has been made into museums.

EMPRESS ELISABETH

Empress Sisi ruled for 44 years.

ERZSEBET KIRÁLYNÉ

While we are at the Hofburg, we can learn about one of Austria's most famous royals. **Empress** Elisabeth, also known as Sisi, ruled Austria longer than any other empress.

She also set up a **dual monarchy** between Austria and Hungary. So, she was also the queen of Hungary.

17

THE ALPS

Now, let's head to nature. The Alps spread across seven countries, including Austria. They make up the largest mountain range in Europe.

More than half of Austria is covered by the Alps. Austria's highest mountain is called Grossglockner. It is almost 12,500 feet (3,800 m) tall.

The Alps started to form even before most dinosaurs lived!

DACHSTEIN CAVES

Time to head underground. The Dachstein Caves are a group of very old underground tunnels. Below the earth here, it is very cold. There is ice all around.

It is so cold that any water in the caves freezes and stays frozen. One cave, called the Dachstein Giant Ice Cave, has ice that is more than 500 years old!

BEFORE YOU GO

Vienna's Ferris wheel has been in a lot of famous movies!

We can't forget to ride Vienna's giant Ferris wheel. It's more than 125 years old. This makes it the oldest Ferris wheel in the world.

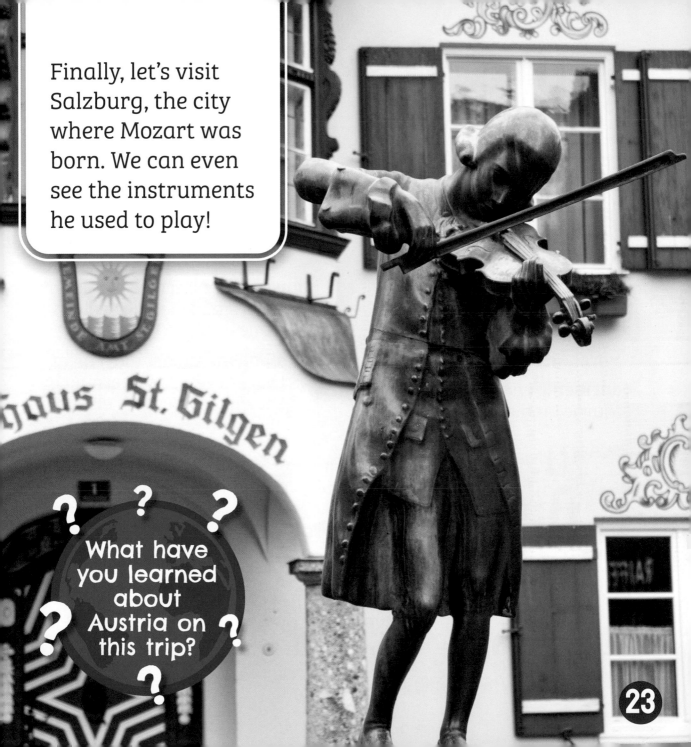

Finally, let's visit Salzburg, the city where Mozart was born. We can even see the instruments he used to play!

What have you learned about Austria on this trip?

23

GLOSSARY

architect a person who designs buildings

borders lines that show where one place ends and another begins

cathedral a very large church

classical a traditional type of music often played by a large orchestra

continent one of the world's seven large land masses

dual monarchy two countries that share the same royal families

empress a woman who rules a country

mosaic a pattern or picture made from small pieces of colorful stone or glass

symbolism an art movement that expresses something by showing something else

INDEX